MW00745030

Through
Family Times

*A Conversational Prayerbook
for Today's World*

by

Ginger Farry

Paulist Press
New York  *Mahwah*

Copyright © 1993 by Ginger Farry

Library of Congress Cataloging-in-Publication Data

Farry, Ginger, 1941–
    Through family times : a conversational prayerbook for today's world / by Ginger Farry.
        p.   cm.
    ISBN 0-8091-3392-X (pbk)
    1. Catholic Church—Prayer-books and devotions—
English.   [1. Family—Prayer-books and devotions—
English.]   I. Title.
BX2170.F3F37   1993
249—dc20   93-15069
                                                           CIP

Published by Paulist Press
997 Macarthur Boulevard
Mahwah, New Jersey 07430

Printed and bound in the
United States of America

For my husband, Jack,
with thanks for his
faith, support, encouragement
and love.

Dear Reader:

In September 1991 my husband lost his job when the company folded. Seven months later, with Jack still unemployed, I was excessed as a teacher. It was not an uncommon occurrence for these times. Some of our closest friends were also facing financial destitution. Even those who had previously been fairly solvent seemed to show signs of monetary stress.

As people of faith, we prayed daily. As people of hope, we gathered together in community. Yet hard times continued. As we became more aware of the needs of others, our desire for discernment and guidance was heightened. Surely God was still there and we were not hearing him or listening closely enough to receive direction.

As always, we turned to the Bible. Trusting in his word was something we had certainly learned to do. But I sighed heavily, as I discovered the reading I had opened to was from Job. To my surprise, however, its message uplifted me.

> You will surely forget your trouble,
> recalling it only as waters gone by.
> Life will be brighter than noonday,
> and darkness will become like morning.
> You will be secure, because there is hope;

you will look about you and take your rest
in safety.
You will lie down, with no one to make
you afraid,
and many will court your favor.

Job 11:16-19

Soon after that, a discussion with my editor, Doug Fisher, brought forth an idea for a new kind of prayer book, one that dealt with the problems of today's world, from joblessness and strife to the everyday stresses of family life, all done in conversational language. I sat down that day and began writing. Because of God's guidance, it didn't take me very long to recall the many issues that are an integral part of family living. Because of God's grace, some of these prayers practically wrote themselves. I hope that my attempt at categorizing them will make it easier for you to find those that pertain to your needs. And I hope that as you read what is here, it will open doors in your personal prayer life, and lead you to rely on his infinite mercy and love.

With praise to his holy name,

Ginger Farry

Prayers for Couples

This is my commandment, that you love one another as I loved you.

John 15:12

We're not talking, Lord,
though there's been no fight,
we're just not connecting—
not seeing your light.

Please help us, dear God,
without accusation,
to engage in the needed
communication.

My spouse and I are down today,
the two of us are lost.
And we can't help each other,
no matter what the cost.

So please, dear Lord, enlighten one,
I beg you, don't refuse
whomever of us you may touch.
Lord, only you can choose.

I'm waiting on you, Lord,
to help one of us to speak.
I'm waiting and praying,
your guidance I seek.

But I have this feeling—
as clear as can be—
and it came in this prayer that:
you're waiting on me!

Today we're angry with each other.
Neither one of us can pray.
Today we're closed,
and cold,
and stubborn,
and I hate to live this way.

And so these words I whisper, Lord,
take away our fault and sin,
and I invite you,
Holy Spirit,
enter in,
oh, enter in.

I wish that he didn't leave angry,
for I can't solve our problems alone,
and yet we need space from each other
(and I need to talk on the phone!)

'Cause my friends offer solace and comfort,
and in them it's no feat to confide,
and I couldn't quite pray at the moment
because of resentment inside.

Yet soon, when the chatter is over,
I'll mellow and come unto you,
regretting the words said in anger,
and knowing just what I should do.

And I'll ask for a heart that's forgiving,
and I'll plead for your spirit and mind,
and finally, at last, when I let you in, Lord,
it's a much gentler spirit I'll find.

And maybe someday I won't tarry
and someday I won't be so late,
and I'll focus on you first, dear Jesus,
so we can omit all the wait!

Thank you, Lord, for today,
for the laughter we shared,
the support we gave one another.

Thank you, too, for our love
and the companionship of our union
forever based in faith.

And lastly, Lord, thanks for our differences
for even though we are not mirrors of one another
—we can be a reflection of you.

I have a critical nature at times
And I tend to see things my way
and because I think of myself as fair
I like what I have to say.

But maybe I'm overly fond of me
and selfishness abounds.
Lord, help me be silent and listen well
until your word resounds.

I almost said the "word" last night
'Cause I know it carries force.
I was so hurt and angry
that I thought about "divorce."
It's not the first time that this option
came into my head;
sometimes when we're not talking, Lord,
I lay awake in bed
and ponder if this marriage
is worth the time and care
'cause when we're in the bad times,
the good ones seem too rare.
And in these moments, it's so hard
to come to you and pray.
It's easier to close the door
and to walk away.

But then I thought about the times,
truth's not an easy stand
and lies might be convenient
and pride too could be grand.
And all the "simpler" things to do
provide a real temptation,
for anger too is easier than
contemplative meditation.
And risking conversation
that comes straight from the heart
requires faith and trust in you
to make another start.

And loving as a Christian
is not an easy task,
but then there's nothing simple, Lord,
about the things you ask.

But if I believe, as 'deed I do,
that, Jesus, you're the light,
then though the journey's difficult,
the path is surely right.
So, Lord, because our union's blessed
—though we get hurt or shout—
because it is your word at stake:
please help us work things out.

Return the newness of love to us, Lord.
Bring back the warmth and affection
that we once shared,
for our feelings are frazzled,
worn by resentment
and trampled by fears.

Give us your eyes, Lord,
with which to see one another.
Give us your heart, Lord,
with which to love.
Give us your Holy Spirit
to open the doors
and lead the way back to each other's arms.

Forgiveness is amazing, Lord,
it more than heals the soul;
it cleanses and refreshes,
it makes a body whole.

And so I come to you right now,
with thanks and joy and praise,
for you helped us through the hard times
and our spirits you did raise.

And even if we fail again,
and sometimes lose our way,
I'll remember what you did for us,
today and every day.

Prayers for Parents

Show thyself in all things an example in good works, in teaching, in integrity and dignity; let thy speech be sound and blameless, so that anyone opposing may be put to shame, having nothing bad to say of us.

Titus 2:7–8

Bottles, books and baby things
strewn across the floor.
Laundry, dishes, cleaning chores—
Lord, there's still much more.

Prayerful time is hard to come by
and quiet moments few.
Yes, I want to be your servant:
but your servant's never through.

So sanctify each task I do,
come join me now, I plead,
for though I need you in my life,
I also need "God's speed."

When they are at school, Lord,
watch over them,
help them listen,
help them learn.

When they play, Lord,
please guide them,
teach them fairness
at each turn.

As they grow, Lord,
protect them,
keep them safe
and strong and free.

For they're yours, Lord,
and you love them;
that's why you gave their care to me.

Latch-Key Kids

Latch-key kids is what they are;
they come and go when I'm not there.
It's not the way I wanted it.
O Lord, you know I care.

So please protect them, Jesus,
for the time they are alone
and rid me of this guilt I feel
when I'm at work and can't be home.

She didn't want to go to church,
she said that she was bored.
I argued and demanded,
so she did it "for me," Lord.

I'm still dismayed and troubled though;
what am I doing wrong?
Or is it just the age she's at—
this "I don't want to" song?

O Lord, please change her heart somehow
and bring her close to you.
I'm weary and I'm worried
and I don't know what to do.

Because someday when I am gone
to meet St. Peter at the gate,
I'd like to know that she'll be there,
'Cause, Lord, I'm gonna wait.

I'm not appreciated, Lord,
by those whom I hold dear;
yes, this is what I feel right now,
this is what I fear:
that I'm taken for granted
and my love they overlook;
I'm simply here to clean the house,
make the beds and cook!
Where's the gratitude, dear Lord?
Where's my consolation?
When has a mother done enough
to receive a commendation?
A simple word of praise and thanks
would make me feel so grand
Oh dear, a . . . never mind, dear Lord,
I think YOU understand!

A Call from College

My daughter's on the phone, dear Lord,
and her needs are very real:
there's textbooks, food and gas expense
in her gentle, sweet appeal.

I pray that we will find the way
to provide her all she asks,
for I know that you too heard her, Lord,
and will help us with these tasks.

And, Jesus, may I now request
that she will recollect,
it would be easier if she "wrote"
and didn't call "collect."

Don't let the world harm them, Lord,
for I know I raised them right;
I taught them to be gentle,
and they don't know how to fight.

That's why sometimes I worry when
they turn the other cheek
that they'll always remember,
you're the power that they seek.

My son is getting married, Lord,
and my daughter is engaged.
I guess I'm growing old, my God.
(Thought I was middle-aged!)
And life is changing rapidly
and adjustments must be made
to handle the emotions
and the memories that won't fade.
Like little tots with bottles
that crawled around the floor,
instead a man and woman
come walking through my door.
And part of me wants to return
to what was long ago,
to hold those little babies
and to never let them go.
But now it's I who have to learn,
and I must come to see,
just like Mary bore your will:
I have to set them free.

*My emotions run the gamut, Lord,
from sadness right through joy.
I'm watching my son marry—
there's no more "baby boy."*

*His bride is young and beautiful,
a new daughter I will gain,
and yet I have this mixture
of happiness and pain.*

*So here's a simple prayer to you
'bout a fear I do deplore:
Help me be a gentle, loving,
silent mother-in-law.*

As they exchange vows, Lord,
watch over them;
help them listen
to each other.

When they dance, Lord,
remind them
that there's one dance
for the mother.

As they leave, Lord,
protect them,
let their love blossom
and grow.

For they're yours, Lord,
and you love them;
that's why I have to let them go.

Stepdaughter

I'm in a funny place, dear Lord,
I'm not her actual mother,
and yet I care about the child,
but as moms go—I'm the "other."

And since she came to stay with us
our lives are different too,
and though I want to help her, Lord,
sometimes I can't get through.

Because we got her very late,
she's not a babe in arms,
and when I make suggestions
I know she has her qualms.

And sometimes it is difficult
since she is not my daughter,
to phrase my words in such a way
that I don't give an "order."

But I have faith that she is here
because it was your plan,
and her dad and I both pray
that we'll do all we can.

And some days, when all goes wrong,
and I find that I am miffed,
Help me recall that she is here
because she is your gift.

A Father's Prayer

Give me the words, Lord,
I ask you,
when it's time for me to speak.
I need to help a child tonight,
so your support I seek.

I've worked all day,
I need my rest,
yet now I must be wise.
Let me see this situation
with your loving eyes.

I'd rather put the TV on
but this problem I must face,
and so I pray you'll aid me
and fill me with your grace.

I'll do my best
to be the dad,
that you want me to be,
but, Lord, I need assistance,
so won't you please help me!

Prayers for Kids

Hear, my son, and receive my words,
and the years of your life shall be many.
On the way of wisdom, I direct you,
I lead you on straightforward paths.
When you walk, your step will not be impeded,
and should you run, you will not stumble.
Hold fast to instruction, never let her go,
keep her, for she is your life.

Proverbs 4:10–13

Lord, I'm in trouble today
for something I didn't do.
I came home late,
I didn't call,
I broke the rules, it's true.

I really know the reason
why they're upset with me;
it seems they always worry
about some tragedy.

But I don't need a lecture
'cause I know just what they'll say.
I kind of want to shut them out,
until this goes away.

So maybe you can reach them, Lord
(I'm really in a spot),
and make them see I'm not so bad—
it's just that "I forgot."

They're not listening, dear Lord,
yet they think that they know
what I should be feeling
and where I should go.

They've made up their minds
'bout what's best for me,
but they're clueless about
my identity.

And I don't have the words
to express what I feel,
and they seem to get angry
when it's just no big deal.

So help them to listen,
and help me to say
what's bubbling inside me—
starting today!

I love the telephone, dear Lord,
it's my communication,
but sometimes when the bill is high
they give me aggravation.

So here comes a simple prayer
but it's straight from my heart:
please help me find a job, Lord,
so I can pay my part!

Thank you for my parents, Lord,
for my home and family.
Thank you for the good things
that you have given me.

Thank you for my friends,
and the good times that we share,
but especially I thank you
because you're always there!

Lord, help me to do well today
at school, and on my test;
clear my mind so I can answer;
I want to do my best.

Guide me and direct me
in everything I say,
and keep me safe, dear Jesus;
this is what I pray.

I believe they want what's best for me
and I believe they care.
I know they wouldn't steer me wrong,
and usually they're fair.

But I've this person deep inside
that's struggling to be free,
to break out and to take a stand
for my identity.

And maybe my confusion
and the turmoil that I'm in
is just because I'm battling
with this person deep within.

So, Lord, please help me focus,
and please help them to see
that as I grow, I'm changing
and discovering "the me."

Whose side are you on, God?
Theirs or mine?
Who's right and who's wrong here?
Can you give me a sign?

Sometimes I'm confused
and I just want to know:
Am I always at fault?
Will I ever grow?

Since you have the answers
to all of my cares,
help them see me through your eyes—
and not with theirs!

My friends don't know I'm praying, Lord;
they might not think it's cool,
but I'm worried 'bout my parents—
keep them safe while I'm at school.

Watch over them, dear Jesus,
don't let them fight or stress.
I know they have their problems
like everyone, I guess.

So I'm asking your assistance
and I hope that you will see:
sometimes I'm scared for them, dear Lord,
and for our family.

And I need someone to talk to
the way we're talking now.
I think it's cool to pray, Lord,
and I pray you'll teach me how.

Lord, I need friendship
and I also need love;
these are the things
that I think the most of.

And I know that you value
the same things I do,
and so that is why
I'm coming to you.

Because you know, Jesus,
that I really believe.
And you said that in giving
we alse receive.

I'm asking you now
to help my heart to mend,
and guide me in finding
a faithful friend.

For Those Who Are Stressed

For God is not the author of confusion, but of peace, as in all churches of the saints.

I Corinthians 14:33

Morning Prayer

My problems woke me early, Lord,
my thoughts are still unclear;
there's so much I must do today,
that's why I'm starting here.

For morning prayer will give me time
to sit and analyze
those worldly woes that bother me,
and view them with your eyes.

And then as I go through my day
I ask you: Stay close by,
so I'll respond with love to all,
and I'll remember why.

I run in directions
that take me from you,
get lost in my problems,
grow saddened and blue.

And sometimes my focus
is scattered, not clear,
and I want to be faith-filled,
yet I'm filled with fear.

O Lord, I need solitude,
silence and prayer,
and as soon as I find them,
oh please meet me there!

There's so much I must do today
and my mind won't stay on track.
I'm forgetting stuff and losing things
and my head's just out of whack.
I've made a list and lost it,
I'm keyed-up as I can be.
O Lord, I need some peaceful prayer
to bring serenity.
And so these simple words I say
to ease my irritation.
Lord, help me keep you in today,
I ask with exclamation!

Overburdened Mom Needs Vacation

How do I solve my dilemma, Lord?
How do I make them see?
I'm trying my best to help them all
and feeling that no one helps me.

And I can't hop a plane to an island,
or sail off on the ocean blue,
so please renew my spirit, Lord,
and let me vacation in you!

I'm angry right now,
and I'm lost in my fears,
for a family disturbance
has moved me to tears.

And though part of me wants
to forgive and forget,
the other part's stubborn
and feels no regret.

So I ask you, dear Lord,
to help me to see,
that insisting "I'm right"
delays change in me.

My in-laws are good people, Lord,
when all is said and done,
but then sometimes I'm in-lawed out
and I just want to run.

Can't take another family fest
or some gala affair;
you see, Lord, I'm in need of rest
from all the wear and tear.

So help me do what I must do,
and heal me where I'm weak,
and hold the obligations—
for at least another week!

There's too many things to do, Lord,
too many thoughts in my head.
I'm scattered and I'm weary,
and I really need to be fed
by your spirit and your power
to ignite me back to life,
to help me face today, Lord,
with its sulleness and strife.
So animate my body, please,
uplift my mental state,
and guide me to a moment's time
where you I'll contemplate.

Lord, help the families
that struggle every day
with pressures, stress and worldly fears:
teach us how to pray.

Renew the family unit
and strengthen ties that bind,
and restore the faith and values
that we need to save mankind.

Tonight I'm a poet
without a rhyme;
tonight I'm too tired
and I don't have the time
to say an appropriate
prayer or two
that might help me grow
ever closer to you.
Tonight my head's empty
and my spirit is weak,
and my eyes are both closing
even now as I speak.
So I just thank you, Lord,
that all is now still,
and I'll see you tomorrow
if that be your will.

I found peace today, Lord,
in the quiet of a chapel
where someone
read your words.

A community of believers
gathered together
to profess
their love.

And you were there, Lord,
in their midst—
of that
I was certain.

And I was both witness
and willing apostle,
a participant
in truth.

For Troubled Times

Praise be to the God and Father of our Lord Jesus Christ, the Father of compassion and the God of all comfort, who comforts us in all our troubles, so that we can comfort those in any trouble with the comfort we ourselves have received from God. For just as the sufferings of Christ flow over into our lives, so also through Christ our comfort overflows.

2 Corinthians 1:3–5

I cannot bear the news, Lord,
and I have to ask you "why"
they're raping little children,
and it makes me want to cry:

The violence, drugs and prejudice,
the unemployment line,
the horror of a murder,
the sadness of each crime.

Deceptive politicians,
the homeless and the poor,
the hungry and the greedy,
are too much to endure.

Yet as my anger heightens, Lord,
I'm silent as a mouse,
not like the day you shouted when
they defiled your Father's house.

And if we must save this world, Lord,
please help me make a stand
for unity of all people
throughout this troubled land.

I'm having trouble loving today, Lord—

*The woman in the supermarket
who yelled at me because
I inadvertently blocked her way . . .*

*The fellow in the red Camaro
who cut me off on the road . . .*

*The telephone solicitor
who insisted I give her
just a few minutes of my time,
as I was putting dinner on the table . . .*

*And even my own dear family
who are presently all too involved
in their own worldly pursuits
to notice my state of mind . . .*

*So here I come in prayer, Lord,
seeking your mercy:
the very same mercy
that today
I was unable to give.*

I'm not feeling well, Lord;
today I am sickly,
and I'm wishing that you
might heal me quickly
because in your love
I know I am wealthy
when it's my time to go:
I'd like to go healthy.

The Prayer That's Always Answered: "Yes"

Help me to be more like you.
Help me to change my heart.
Help me to walk in justice, to be gentle.
Help me start.

Help me to be humble, Lord,
not critical or coarse.
Will you help me become better, Lord?
You will, of course, of course!

One of your people hurt me today,
one of your people was cruel.
I didn't expect it, it came as a shock,
for we were co-workers at school.

I guess there is no one who's perfect but you,
and all of us fall now and then.
It's just that I didn't expect to be hurt
by someone whom I called a friend.

It took me a while to forgive and forget,
forty-eight hours or so,
and now that it's over, I'm writing this poem
and then I am letting it go.

The closer I come to your people, Lord,
the more my eyes can see.
It isn't their worldly traits I view,
it's their humanity.

Life seems so unfair at times
when we lose someone we love.
To have to say goodbye to them
is the last thing we dreamt of.

We're empty and we're broken,
confused and angry too,
and if you stood before us, Lord,
we'd like to question you.

But something deep inside us
is saying through our tears:
"I understand your sorrow,
I understand your fears."

Perhaps it's Mother Mary,
who surely knows our pain,
for she's the Queen of Sorrows
who can lead us home again.

And help us come to terms with all
the suffering in "farewell"
so we may grow through sadness
and impede that aching swell.

For though we're truly hurting
as the separation grows,
as Christians we know "goodbyes"
are followed by "hellos."

Saying goodbye for a week, month or year
may cause us a little misgiving.
But having life change its course in midstream
is part of the process of living.

Looking for strength when our well has run dry
may challenge our patience in prayer.
But learning to soar on eagles' wings
is possible—for you are there.

Goodbye, St. Agnes

I have to say goodbye, Lord,
to the girls I came to love,
the students that I prayed for
and thought the whole world of!

I have to leave them now, Lord,
and walk a different road,
and I don't know where I'm going
so it seems a heavy load.

But somehow you are present
even as I write this prayer,
and I know that you'll be with them, Lord,
for I know how much you care.

So grant them peace and safety,
protect them, Jesus, please,
and help them do their homework.
(THIS, I ask you on my knees!)

And may the many paths they choose
be guided by your light,
and may they make a difference
in this world that's not yet right.

And let them keep you in their hearts
for all to know and see,
that when our lives are touched by faith,
we form: community.

Lord of My Senses

I strolled along the beach today,
in solitude and prayer,
listening to the breaking waves—
I felt your presence there.

I walked along in silence,
saw your splendor in the sky,
and I was touched, dear Jesus,
though I'm not sure that I know why.

I breathed the salty air and sensed
the slowness of my pace,
and then at last, I realized,
your goodness I could taste.

For Those with Financial Worries

Therefore I say to you, do not be anxious for your life, what you shall eat; nor yet for your body, what you shall put on. Is not the life a greater thing than the food, and the body than the clothing? Look at the birds of the air: they do not sow, or reap, or gather into barns; yet your heavenly Father feeds them. Are not you of much more value than they? But which of you by being anxious about it can add to his stature a single cubit?

And as for clothing, why are you anxious? Consider how the lilies of the field grow; they neither toil or spin, yet I say to you that not even Solomon in all his glory was arrayed like one of these. But if God so clothes the grass of the field, which flourishes today but tomorrow is thrown into the oven, how much more you, O you of little faith.

Matthew 6:25–30

I'm worried about money, Lord,
for the mortgage and the bills.
I know about the lilies,
and the birds upon the hills.

So I guess I should be patient
and place my trust in you,
for then, of course, I'd realize:
With me you're not quite through!

It's summertime, Lord,
and the kids have no school,
and they're running me ragged
to buy them a pool.

And though I agree
that it would be a treat,
finding the money
would be a real feat.

So I'm saying this prayer
for my son and daughter.
Could you help us, Lord,
and lead us to water!

My friend needs a job,
and, Lord, so do I,
and another friend's sick
and I just want to cry
'cause this woman with cancer
has asked me to pray,
and my daughter at college
requested I pay
for the books and tuition,
and I haven't a clue
how to handle the sorrow
and vicissitude too.
And a couple I know
has just filed for divorce,
and a friend of a friend
has a child who is lost.
And each problem I hear
makes me quiver and shake—
so I give them to you, Lord,
or else I might break.

I love the day when you were born,
and all the Christmas flair.
I love the season's spirit
and the carols in the air.

I love to watch the faces
of the little ones I know,
to see their jubilation,
their bright eyes all aglow.

But the holidays grow frenzied, Lord
and shopping gets me down.
I seem to lose perspective
and my smile becomes a frown.

Financial pressures play a part,
commercialism reigns—
instead of celebrating you,
we proclaim capital gains!

So, Lord, please help us focus in
on meaning—only one—
a child is born, a King arrives.
He's Jesus Christ, the Son.

We depend on you, Lord,
for all our needs,
and though some think it funny,
we know that whenever funds are low,
you always send the money.

It comes from sources we forgot,
from faraway places too.
But no matter how it comes, dear Lord,
we know it comes from you!

Prayers for the Unemployed

For the rest, brethren, be strengthened in the Lord and in the might of his power. Put on the armor of God, that you may be able to stand against the wiles of the devil. For our wrestling is not against flesh and blood, but against the Principalities and the Powers, against the world-rulers of this darkness, against the spiritual forces of wickedness on high. Therefore take up the armor of God, that you may be able to resist in the evil day, and stand in all things perfect. Stand, therefore, having girded your loins with truth, and having put on the breastplate of justice, and having your feet shod with the readiness of the gospel of peace, in all things taking up the shield of faith with which you may be able to quench all the fiery darts of the most wicked one. And take unto you the helmet of salvation, and the sword of the spirit, that is, the word of God.

Ephesians 6:10–17

I toss and turn, Lord,
as fears invade my faith,
sleepless nights
as cold as the snow.

Yet surely I can depend upon you for my needs.
Surely you will not let me down.
In the spirit, I can sing to you,
yet my flesh longs to be warmed by your grace.

Let the glow from your undying love caress me,
let me rest in the safety of your compassion,
for indeed YOU are at work, Lord,
and will help me find a job.

Where will I go today, Lord?
And what will I do?
The classified section
supplies no clue.

Humbly, Lord, I look to you.

I began with mass this morning
seeking sacramental grace.
I struggled through some daily chores
and tried to set a pace
to stretch out my activities
to last the whole day long.
And then I read a while, dear Lord,
and hummed a cheerful song.
But soon the stress within my heart
attacked my plan of hope,
and I became dejected
and my mind just couldn't cope.
So I tried to give you thanks, Lord,
counted blessings through my tears,
and I thought of how you care for me
in spite of all my fears.
But sorrow still invaded me,
and I can't deny what's real,
nor would you want me to pretend
about the way I feel.
For my heart is very heavy,
and it's difficult to pray.
I need a job, dear Jesus,
and my family needs my pay.
So help the lost-ness in me,
and help me not forget
the promises you've made, Lord,

for good is coming yet.
And all the pleas I've muttered
to heaven up above
have been heard by you, my Savior,
in your unfailing love.

The Interview

Calm me down, Lord,
as I wait.
Let your spirit
permeate
through my body, heart and mind,
so I'll relax
and I'll unwind.
Give me words
to tell them true,
that I'm good
but humble too.
And, finally,
please help me see
that you have
a plan for me
And if this job
is not the one,
Jesus, Lord,
your will be done.

A Matter of Image

Some people looked at me today
and didn't like what they saw.
They judged me by appearance.
(Have I judged like that before?)

It felt strange to be rejected.
I felt the coldness of their stare.
I wanted to say "Don't judge me like this,
'cause I really don't think it's fair."

But I walked away without comment,
and, Jesus, I know it's true,
that prejudice comes in many forms—
that's why they rejected you!

I didn't get the job, Lord,
and I can't imagine why,
but I'll accept your will in this
(though I think I'm going to cry) . . .

And I hope it went to someone
needier than I.

Another interview, dear Lord
(and I was feeling blue),
another possibility—
is this one from you?

I was really quite dejected,
now my spirits all have soared,
and I trust my unknown future
to a known and loving Lord.

For Discernment

For this reason I bend my knees to the Father of our Lord Jesus Christ, from whom all fatherhood in heaven and on earth receives its name, that he may grant you from his glorious riches to be strengthened with power through his Spirit unto the progress of the inner man; and to have Christ dwelling through faith in your hearts: so that you may be able to comprehend with all the saints what is the breadth and length and height and depth, and to know Christ's love which surpasses knowledge, in order that you may be filled unto all the fullness of God.

Ephesians 3:16–19

How will I hear you today, Lord?
Will your word come loud and strong?
Will it bellow from a TV show
or echo in a song?

Will it come from friend or loved one?
A stranger? Someone's boss?
Lord, I'll be listening for you:
no matter what the source.

Each day I ask for guidance, Lord,
though I stumble and I fall.
I try to keep an open heart
and listen for your call.

Perhaps I haven't learned enough
or maybe it's not time,
for in seeking out direction:
Do the branches ask the vine?

Or do they simply grow as one,
naturally and free?
I know I'll find the way, dear Lord,
if I keep you in me.

Today it's a little clearer, Lord,
and I think I know what to do;
I'm not going to seek "an experience"
but, rather, I'll seek you.

How often I sought you, Lord,
asking, pleading, yearning
for your intervention.
How often I pondered you, Lord,
in the path of personal direction.

In the desert of my life I searched for you,
calling you "problem solver" and "keeper of my soul."
But you did not come to solve my problems, Lord.
You came to make me whole.

Pure Joy

Sometimes you shine through my children,
I can see you in laughter and pain.
Sometimes you're present in strangers,
and always in sunshine and rain.

What a comfort it is, dearest Jesus,
to see you in others each day,
and to note all the joy, the peace, and the strength
that's ours when we follow your way.

And it seems like we're sharing a secret,
one you once asked that we not tell,
and we're shouting it from the rooftops:
O Lord, you know us well!

Prayers of Thanksgiving

And it shall come to pass, that before they call, I will answer; and while they are yet speaking, I will hear."

Isaiah 65:24

I found peace in my kitchen today
among the pots and pans.
I sang a tune and danced around
and even clapped my hands.

And I think I know the reason
why nothing was the same:
I recalled the many good things
that are mine with just your name!

Thank you for nature, thank you for joy,
thank you for children, each girl and each boy,
thank you for beauty in all we behold,
than you for truth, whenever it's told.

Thank you for friends, for work and for play,
thanks for tomorrow and for yesterday,
thank you for animals, thank you for love,
thank you for making heaven above.

Thank you for music and thank you for dreams,
thank you for listening to our silly schemes,
thank you for prayers that are always heard,
and thank you, dear Lord, for giving your word.

Thank you, Lord, for your gifts,
for this day, and for my family.

Thank you for your graces
and the many blessings you've given us.

But especially, Lord,
thank you for words,
especially words of thanks.